Science at home

QUESTIONS

PUBLISHING
COMPANY

Science at home

Practical activities for parents and children

John Stringer

THE QUESTIONS PUBLISHING COMPANY LTD
BIRMINGHAM
2000

First published in 2000 by
The Questions Publishing Company Ltd
27 Frederick Street, Birmingham B1 3HH

Designed by Al Stewart
Edited by Diane Parkin
Illustrations by Sue Woollatt, Graham-Cameron Illustration
Cover design by Lisa Martin

ISBN: 1-84190-027-3

Contents

Introduction

Why homework?

P<small>ARENTS</small> are enthusiastic about helping children with their homework. It's easy to see possible reasons for this. Helping your children with their homework:

- demonstrates your own interest in their progress;
- demonstrates that you know that schoolwork is important;
- can give you a chance to demonstrate your own knowledge and enthusiasm;
- may give you an opportunity to work together on an enjoyable activity;
- reassures you that your child is doing 'real' work at school.

Parents and carers and homework

Experience shows that while parents like this stake in their child's learning, some may be unreliable – even apparently feckless – in maintaining their side of the arrangement. Why should this be?

There are a number of parents who feel that if the school is doing its job, there's no need for additional homework. Among those are some who give their children related experiences – visits, books, computer resources – that relate to schoolwork, or that are simply worthwhile activities.

There are others who start out willingly, but find that family pressures and shortness of time mean that the homework becomes a chore. We can sympathise with them.

Some may find the homework baffling; it may be difficult, or couched in unfamiliar phrases, or just not what they remember from school. Among these are some who question homework if it doesn't resemble their definition of schoolwork.

It is up to the school to get the homework right. There is a world of difference between sending home a page of sums (worthwhile, if it saves lesson time that could be spent on something more productive) and sending something that makes direct use of the opportunities presented by the home environment:

- varied resources;
- opportunities for practical work;
- opportunities for long-term investigations;
- one-to-one teaching.

The pupil sheets

The aim of this book is to exploit these opportunities through a set of activities that are directly relevant to home. The activities are intended to be stimulating and varied; and to set up a dialogue with the parents in which all parties gain – especially the child.

You might decide to send a general letter in advance of the first homework sheets. Explain that:

- the sheets are supporting the children's learning at school;
- they will be essentially practical, using materials from home;
- you would like to involve parental support because they can work closely with a child, encouraging his or her thinking and planning;
- you welcome feedback. Investigations are not wholly predictable or foolproof; but you can assure them that the planned activities will not make a mess of the kitchen.

Page layout

The headings used on the photocopiable pupil pages are as follows:

Title

Child's name:

Date activity set: Here you can put the date you give out the work.

Date for returning this sheet to school: Give children – and parents – an idea of when you are expecting a reply.

To the parent or adult carer: This paragraph explains what the activity is setting out to do. There is space here for safety advice and practical suggestions – like how to ensure good-sized bubbles.

What to do: This paragraph explains the activity. Writing to an adult carer gives an opportunity to invite mediation of the homework.

What to talk about: There's a chance for parent and child to discuss the outcomes. Some of them may be novel to an adult too.

What to record: "Record", not write. Acknowledging that there are several ways of recording science and mathematics outcomes, this paragraph applies them to real life. The child could write or draw; the parent or carer could act as a scribe; there's no reason why tape or disc outcomes should not be produced.

Comment from parent or carer: A chance for them to come back to you. Is the task pitched too high, or too low? Is the relevance not seen, or are the skills not appreciated? It takes courage to read the feedback; often the response can be upsetting. Distance yourself from remarks like 'This was a waste of time' and ask yourself whether the parent is clear on the purpose of (say) investigative mathematics. Maybe the 'page of sums' mentality needs addressing – perhaps through the school's home/school communications, or a meeting of parents.

From the teacher: Here's a chance for you to reply if you want to. At least the parents can see that you have read and registered their work with their child. At best, you might start a real dialogue that sees both of you working even more closely for the child's benefit.

Finally, select homework tasks with the advantages of home in mind. In the home environment, plants can be grown over a period of time, changes observed in the night sky, measurements made of growing, changing children. Above all, a working relationship can be established or enhanced that is of mutual benefit.

A fine teacher once said that in his opinion, an hour spent with a parent could be worth a term with a child. The creative use of homework can support this sort of development.

1 Investigation

Teachers' notes

Scientific washing-up

This is a familiar activity that supports work in Sc1 – science investigations – of the 'what shall we change; what shall we measure; what shall we keep the same?' variety. While the outcome – really hot water with a squirt of detergent – is familiar to everyone with experience of washing-up, the reasons may not be. Detergents help water to wet surfaces; and they help hold the dirt in suspension.

Value for money

This introduces a mathematics investigation with a debatable outcome. While it can be quite easy to work out the cost per hundred grams of a range of soap and detergent products, this is not a measure of value for money – unless low price is your only criterion. There are packets of micro-detergents available which sell on being small, light to carry and containing concentrated detergent.

Keeping food

A kitchen supplies plenty of examples of food storage. Apart from the ones listed on the sheet, you might expect children to come up with pickling – where the acid conditions prevent the growth of bacteria. Or jams and preserves, where sealing while hot, and the high sugar content which dehydrates microbes by osmosis (except when water collects under the lid, drips into the jam, and encourages the growth of a 'fur coat') keeps the fruit.

How long?

This mathematics exercise, which leads to a bar chart, is not a measure of the 'best before' date, but rather of storage times. Figures like 'up to six months in a freezer' are common; but times for chilled and fresh use may be given, yielding three or more figures for one product. The graph could have adjoining or overlapping columns for this eventuality.

Plant types

Research has shown that even older children are not clear on what constitutes a plant, or that familiar plants (trees, for example) are alive. This sheet introduces the main groups, points out that fungi are not plants, and asks for anything from a series of pictures to a branching key to identify the plants. Lichens may be introduced by some; they are a symbiotic pairing of fungi and algae.

How many?

This is an exercise in the useful skill of sampling – which finds applications in both mathematics and science. Children are asked to estimate the number of pulses or other seeds in a container – using a sample. This can find practical applications in natural science – in the estimation of numbers of plants in an area – or even the number of animals in large flocks and groups.

White powder mystery

This is a bit of fun that works on many levels. The idea is to take some safe kitchen powders – all foods – and to identify them in any way except by tasting. It takes careful observational skills, and maybe a bit of adding to water. You could supplement it at school by using a binocular microscope to show magnified crystals. The crystals of salt and sugar are very different, while the crystals of artificial sweetener can be needle-like. An interesting follow-up can be to explore why cans of cola sink, while diet cola cans float. Is it because of the cans? Or the contents?

Bursting bubbles

You can blow bubbles with almost anything, given a dilute detergent solution and some very clean materials. Adding some glycerine to the mixture makes the bubbles last longer. As each bubble nears bursting, it changes colour in a predictable pattern – the result of the changing effects of the thinning bubble skin on light. The moment before bursting, the bubble turns black, momentarily. At this point, the skin is probably only a molecule thick.

Exploring decay

This sheet looks at the way that bread decays. Moist, warm conditions encourage mould growth; and this accounts for some unusual findings – that unwrapped bread lasts longer than wrapped bread would; the wrapping keeps it warm and moist. Remember to give clear safety advice, since a very few people are allergic to mould spores.

Scientific washing-up

Child's name:

Date activity set:

Date for returning this sheet to school:

To the parent or adult carer:
This could be done to enliven washing-up – or you can be more scientific by providing specially soiled plates. The point is to find what combination of methods cleans crockery best – scientifically.

Detergents help water to shift grease. Do not use water hotter than water from the hot tap.

SAFETY: Do not handle or allow children to handle or sniff detergents, especially biological powders or detergents used with dishwashers, both of which can be harmful.

What to do:
Time to wash up. But what method does it as well as a dishwasher?
You could wash the plates:

- by rinsing in clean cold water;
- by rinsing in clean hot water;
- by rubbing in clean cold water;
- by rubbing in clean hot water;
- by rinsing in clean cold water with a drop of detergent;
- by rinsing in clean hot water with a drop of detergent;
- by rubbing in clean cold water with a drop of detergent;
- by rubbing in clean hot water with a drop of detergent.

What to talk about:
Which method worked best? Why do you think that was? Was your test fair? How could you make it fairer?

What to record:
The school kitchen can't keep up with the dirty plates. On the back of this sheet, tell them the best way to do the washing-up.

Comment from parent or carer:

From the teacher:

Value for money

Child's name:

Date activity set:

Date for returning this sheet to school:

To the parent or adult carer:
Detergents, soaps and washing powders have a weight printed on the box or bottle. This can be used, together with the price, to compare different-sized containers. You may use the 'price per kilogram' labels on supermarket shelves when you shop.

What to do:
Look at the weights and prices on a collection of soap and detergent products.

SAFETY: Do not handle or allow children to handle or sniff detergents, especially biological powders or detergents used with dishwashers, both of which can be harmful.

What to talk about:
Where are the weights? What do they mean? Where are the prices? Put them in the first three columns of this table:

Product	Weight	Price	Price for 100 grams

Now divide to give you a price per hundred grams for the last column.

Is this a measure of value for money? Can you compare these products directly? Probably not. There is quality to take into account; and smaller measures of more expensive powders can do a better job than larger ones of cheap.

What to record:
Advise someone on the 'Best Buy' soap or detergent if price is the only important factor to them. Tell them why price may not be the only thing to look at.

Comment from parent or carer:

From the teacher:

Keeping food

Child's name:

Date activity set:

Date for returning this sheet to school:

To the parent or adult carer:
If food is not properly stored, it rots quickly. We use different methods of storing food – from vegetable racks to let the air circulate around fresh food, to deep freezes to keep food for long periods. The bacteria and moulds that cause food to rot grow best in warm, damp conditions.

What to do:
Look around the kitchen. Complete this table:

Name of food I saw:	This food is:
	Fresh
	Dried
	Canned
	Chilled
	Frozen

What to talk about:
Which food will last the longest? Why is this? What happens to fresh food? Will this happen to the other foods, in time?

What to record:
A gardener has too many apples to eat. Give some ideas for keeping the rest of the apples for as long as possible. Put all the ideas you can on the back of this sheet.

Comment from parent or carer:

From the teacher:

How long?

Child's name:

Date activity set:

Date for returning this sheet to school:

To the parent or adult carer:
Many foods have a recommended keeping time on the packet. This may vary for fresh, chilled or frozen food.

What to do:
Collect together some food packets – don't keep frozen food out for long – and record the keeping times. Note the times for different types of fridge and freezer – sometimes listed on a star scale.

Draw a block graph of the keeping times of different foods. Put the names of the foods along the horizontal (x) axis, and the time up the vertical (y) axis.

You may need to put more than one graph on top of another. One product may have a keeping time fresh; another time in the fridge; and a third time in the freezer.

What to talk about:
What do your results show? Does freezing actually stop decay; or only slow it down? Why is it dangerous to eat out-of-date food?

What to record:
A friend is going on a camping trip. Advise on foods which will keep a long time without a fridge or freezer.

A neighbour has just bought a freezer, and asks you for some foods that will keep a long time in it.

Let both these people know which foods to choose.

Comment from parent or carer:

From the teacher:

Plant types

Child's name:

Date activity set:

Date for returning this sheet to school:

To the parent or adult carer:
Many children do not know that both daffodils and seaweed are plants. Some do not realise that trees are living plants. Use a garden or the local park to discover the different kinds of plants. Fungi are not considered to be part of the plant kingdom.

What to do:
Use a place with plenty of plants – and a pond or stream, too.
Complete this table:

Type	I saw
Green, flowering plants	
Trees – large green, flowering plants	
Mosses – plants with spores	
Algae – pond weeds, seaweeds	
Fungi – not plants at all	

Perhaps you could draw one.

What to talk about:
What makes something a plant? Do plants hunt and eat food? Where do they get their food from? Not from the ground. Do they make it themselves? Find out how they use sunlight to make food from water and carbon dioxide in the air.

What to record:
On the back of this sheet, show a gardener how to tell the different sorts of plant apart.

Comment from parent or carer:

From the teacher:

How many?

Child's name:

Date activity set:

Date for returning this sheet to school:

To the parent or adult carer:
This is a sampling activity. It helps children to see that we can count huge numbers by sampling small ones. You could use any dry pulse food for it – dried peas, beans, or even some seed spices – like peppercorns.

What to do:
Challenge the child to count all the peas in the packet. How long would it take? If you only want an approximate number, you can find it by sampling.

Use an appropriate spoon or measure. Fill one spoonful. Count the peas in one spoonful. Now count the number of spoonfuls in the packet – and multiply up. You might need a calculator.

What to talk about:
How accurate is this method? Why might it be better to take more than one spoonful – and average them?

Could you use a similar method to count sheets of paper? Packages?

Some packets have 'average contents' written on them. What does this mean? How could you check?

What to record:
A gardener wants to know how many flowers she has in her garden. Tell her how she could do it by counting the plants in one small square.

Comment from parent or carer:

From the teacher:

White powder mystery

Child's name:

Date activity set:

Date for returning this sheet to school:

To the parent or adult carer:
Put some white powder foods – salt, sugar, flour, caster sugar, sweetener – on separate saucers. Ask your child how to name each one – without tasting. Ideas might include careful sniffing, feeling with fingers, adding to water, even looking at crystals with a magnifying glass.

What to do:
Here are some mystery powders. You are asked to name them. You can try any safe test. You can't taste the powders; after all, they could be anything. Plan some simple tests. Try to name the powders. Ask. Were you right?

What to talk about:
What differences are there? How do they feel, look, smell, behave in water?

What to record:
A scientist asks you for a simple test to recognise salt and sugar. Explain how you can do this correctly – every time.

Comment from parent or carer:

From the teacher:

Bursting bubbles

Child's name:

Date activity set:

Date for returning this sheet to school:

To the parent or adult carer:
This is a bit of fun that also teaches children about investigating in science.

You can make a good bubble mixture with a small amount of washing-up liquid in water. If you can add a drop of glycerine, the bubbles will last longer. Put the mixture in a low, wide container like a casserole. You can blow bubbles with anything. Try loops of garden wire, boxes with both ends open, kitchen roll tubes.

What to do:
Answer these questions:

● Can you change the shape of bubbles? Do square blowers blow cubic bubbles?
● Who can blow the biggest bubble? How did you do it?
● How can you predict the moment when a bubble will burst? How does the bubble change colours?
● Can you blow a bubble on a surface – on the kitchen top, for example? How long does it last?

What to talk about:
The changes you made and how the bubbles changed as a result. Link what you did with what you saw.

What to record:
You are asked for advice on blowing the world's biggest bubble. What do you advise? Put your suggestions on the back of this sheet.

Comment from parent or carer:

From the teacher:

Exploring decay

Child's name:

Date activity set:

Date for returning this sheet to school:

To the parent or adult carer:
You are asked to let some bread go mouldy. This is going to take at least a week – perhaps as long as a fortnight. It is very important that you seal the bread in small polythene bags; and that you throw the bags, unopened, into the dustbin afterwards. There is a tiny chance of growing something harmful; and some people are allergic to mould spores.

What to do:
Cut a slice of bread in two. Toast one half. Cut your bread into small cubes. Treat each one differently. Here are some ideas:

- a fresh bread cube;
- a toasted bread cube;
- a damp bread cube;
- a damp toast cube;
- a buttered bread cube;
- a buttered toast cube.

You will think of some more.

Put each cube in a small plastic bag, and seal it with a wire; or wrap each one loosely in cling film.

Leave your cubes somewhere warm. Look at them every day.

What to talk about:
What are the best conditions for making things decay? What are the best conditions for keeping food for a time?

What to record:
Your friends want to take bread on a camping trip. On the back of this sheet, show them how to keep the bread in the best condition.

Comment from parent or carer:

From the teacher:

2 Life processes

Teachers' notes

On the window-sill

Plants grow towards the Sun, and a plant on a sunny window-sill will align its leaves so as to catch the most sunlight. The reason for this – that the leaf is the plant's food factory using the power of sunlight – can be introduced. A mirror – even one made of tinfoil – will reflect the light, balancing the sunlight falling on the plant. The plant should grow upright, with horizontal leaves.

Planting seeds

Plants need the right conditions – light, warmth, moisture – to grow well. This activity looks at these needs in the context of home. Children could compare their results and their successes or failures.

Growing bulbs

Another home-growing activity. Special bulbs are not essential – an onion will shoot in the right conditions – but you could buy a bag of small bulbs or corms and give the children one each as a starter.

How many blades of grass?

This activity looks at the whole business of counting large numbers – a valuable skill in many natural history enquiries. A sample area is multiplied up to get a figure for a large space.

The ladybird game

How many is a good sample? You can't always count the lot; so here is a way of working from a sample. This is a good activity for adults, too; and another way of doing it might be for a child to prepare it for a parent to try.

Making a change

Investigations with living things are difficult; so here's a way of making a modest change – covering a small part of a lawn – to see what takes place. Be aware of children who may not have access to grass.

Mini-safari

By exploring the changes that take place from one end of the string to another, the children are reminded that there are 'mini-habitats' where small local changes result in a different flora and fauna.

On the window-sill

Child's name:

Date activity set:

Date for returning this sheet to school:

To the parent or adult carer:
This activity focuses on the importance of light to the growth of plants. Plants grown on the window-sill will bend towards the light to catch as much as possible on their leaves; they need this light to grow.

Putting a mirror behind the plants will even out the light, and they will grow more upright, with the leaves closer to horizontal.

What to do:
Plant some seeds; cress seeds on moist paper towel will do fine, and grow very quickly.

Put the growing seedlings on a sunny window-sill; keep them moist and check on how they grow.

Notice any changes to the way the seedlings grow. Turn them around. How will this change the way they grow?

Make a mirror from cooking foil. Put the mirror the other side of the plants from the window, so that it reflects the light.

What do you observe over the next few days?

What to talk about:
What happens to the plant growth; and why the plants need light.

What to record:
A flower arranger needs tall, straight plants for a display. Tell her how to get the plants to grow straight up. Use the back of this paper.

Comment from parent or carer:

From the teacher:

Planting seeds

Child's name:

Date activity set:

Date for returning this sheet to school:

To the parent or adult carer:
Plant some seeds, and grow the plants. You could buy the seeds, or collect them from garden plants. Grow them in different conditions. If you want quick results, use cress, mung beans, or alfalfa. Otherwise the activity will take some time. Follow the growing instructions on the seed packet. Grow the plants on a sunny window-sill. Draw your child's attention to all the changes taking place.
If you grow a food plant, you could always wash and eat the results.

What to do:
Grow some plants. Grow two lots of plants, in different conditions. You might:

- grow some on the window-sill, some in a cupboard;
- grow some in a warm place, some in a cold one;
- water some every day, and some every week;
- grow some in compost, and some in garden soil;
- give some fertiliser, and some not.

Observe the changes that take place. Talk about them. Record them in a diary or on a calendar.

What to talk about:
What changes did you see? When did they happen? Which were the better conditions for growth? Why do you think that was?

What to record:
You have had some messages from disappointed gardeners. Tell them the best way to make their plants grow well. Put your ideas on the back of this sheet.

Comment from parent or carer:

From the teacher:

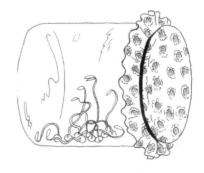

Growing bulbs

Child's name:

Date activity set:

Date for returning this sheet to school:

To the parent or adult carer:
You are asked to grow a bulb. You might grow it inside, over water (as you do with hyacinths) to show your child the roots growing, too. You don't need a special hyacinth grower if you can balance the bulb on a wide-necked bottle. The roots must reach the water.

Draw your child's attention to the changes as the plant grows. If possible, save the dead flower head, cut it open, and show that the plant also produces seeds.

What to do:
Grow a bulb. A bulb contains all the food stores a plant needs to grow at first; then it makes its own food, using sunlight, water and carbon dioxide from the air.

Observe your plant regularly. Keep a record of how it changes in a diary or on a calendar.

What to talk about:
What changes did you see? When did you see the first leaves, a bud, the flower? Did you give the plant anything except water? Where did all the growth come from? Does your plant produce seeds?

What to record:
Cut an onion bulb in half, from top to bottom. Draw what you see inside. Use your drawing to explain what happens as bulbs grow.

Comment from parent or carer:

From the teacher:

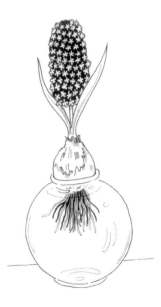

How many blades of grass?

Child's name:

Date activity set:

Date for returning this sheet to school:

To the parent or adult carer:
This is an activity to do with sampling. Often it's impossible to count very large numbers of things, but you can take a sample and multiply up. This is especially useful when looking at the natural world.

This sheet asks you to choose some plants in a garden or open ground, and to use sampling to estimate how many there are. Accuracy is not important; the method is.

What to do:
Find a place with lots of the same plant growing. They might be garden plants or weeds. How long would it take you to count all of them?

Take a small area. Count the plants there. How many times will your small area fit into the garden? What multiplication sum will you have to do to estimate the number of plants in the whole garden?

Can you estimate the answer?

What to talk about:
Suppose you sampled an area that had far fewer plants than most places – or far more. Why would your estimate be a poor one?

What to record:
A gardener friend pulls five dandelions from a square metre of his lawn. The lawn is 8m by 9m. Estimate how many dandelions he has got to dig up altogether. Then tell him how to estimate the number of daisies in the lawn.

Comment from parent or carer:

From the teacher:

The ladybird game

Child's name:

Date activity set:

Date for returning this sheet to school:

To the parent or adult carer:
It's very hard to count animals in the wild. This is a game that helps your child understand how to find the size of a population by sampling. It's a technique used in all kinds of surveys.

You will need to prepare some 'ladybirds' in advance, and in secret. Cut or tear up twenty or more pieces of paper. Put spots on them; ten with two spots, five with three spots, five with four spots. Scatter them all under a newspaper or cloth.

What to do:
The newspaper represents a plant. You are going to estimate how many ladybirds live on the plant. You can't see them all.

Reach under the newspaper. Pull out one ladybird. How many spots has it? Pull out another ladybird. How many spots has this one?

Go on pulling out ladybirds until you think you can tell: how many sorts of ladybird there are; how many of each sort there are; how many ladybirds there are altogether.

Then lift the newspaper. Were you right?

What to talk about:
Is it a good idea to make very early guesses? Can you be misled? Try again, with a different population. Are you better at it this time?

What to record:
Some bird-watchers want to count the different ducks on a lake. They can only see part of the lake at a time. Tell them how to do it.

Comment from parent or carer:

From the teacher:

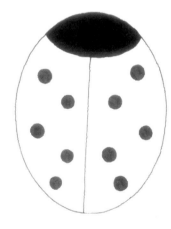

Making a change

Child's name:

Date activity set:

Date for returning this sheet to school:

To the parent or adult carer:
This is an activity that you need to start straight away, so that you can have some results in a week or so.

Putting something on some grass, or covering a plant or a window box, changes the conditions. Your child is asked to record the 'before-and-after' effects of changing living conditions.

What to do:
Cover a small part of a lawn. You could use a carpet square, a tile or an old piece of wood. Look carefully before you cover the area. What is growing there? What does it look like?

Wait a week. Lift the cover carefully. What do you see? How have the plants changed? Are there animals under the cover? Why do you think that is?

What to talk about:
What changes did you make to the light, the temperature, the wetness or dryness? Why did this lead to the changes you saw?

What to record:
Draw what you saw under the cover – before and after – on the back of this sheet.

Comment from parent or carer:

From the teacher:

Mini-safari

Child's name:

Date activity set:

Date for returning this sheet to school:

To the parent or adult carer:
By looking closely, children can become more aware of the range and diversity of living things. This activity uses a length of string as a 'safari trail'. Run a few metres of string across a garden or some clean, safe rough ground. If you put the string across changing conditions – into a flower bed or across a well-worn path – then you can relate the changed conditions to the different plants and animals.

What to do:
The string is a safari trail. Follow the trail, keeping close to the ground. Go slowly. Look for all the plants and animals. You could use a magnifying glass to help you imagine you were only a few centimetres high.

Notice what happens to the plants and animals when conditions change.

What to talk about:
What did you see? Why are there different plants and animals in different places?

What to record:
Tell the story of your mini-safari. Show the plants and animals you came across on the way. Maybe draw a map of your journey on the back of this sheet.

Comment from parent or carer:

From the teacher:

3 Materials

Teachers' notes

Test your soil

This sheet introduces the idea of there being differences between soils. Parents can take it as far as they like; they may have their own test kits for acidity. But it is enough to recognise that soils vary in their properties.

The power of peat

Peat has remarkable water-retention qualities; and this activity enables parents and children to test these in some garden peat. The activity can be used to support the concept that plants make their own food.

Solid clay

This sheet looks at clay as a natural material that can be changed (reversibly) by drying and, (irreversibly) by heat.

Bubbling and peeling

This sheet looks at the way that materials decay by asking children to find examples of Sun damage around their home. There may also be examples of corrosion.

Rotting and rusting

Focusing especially on the corrosion of metals. An investigation into what makes iron-based metals rust. Note that water alone is not enough; oxygen must also be present.

The rustiest nail

This is a challenge that highlights the conditions needed for rusting. You can stimulate the activity by providing small, safe metal objects to test; large paper clips, for example.

Test your soil

Child's name:

Date activity set:

Date for returning this sheet to school:

To the parent or adult carer:
Soils vary in their qualities. This is difficult for children to grasp – they may just see dirt as dirt. But you will know differently if you have tried to grow plants in a garden, allotment or window-box.

You will need samples of earth from two different places.

What to do:
Examine two or more samples of earth. How many differences can you see?
Try squeezing the earth. Does it hold together? Or does it crumble and fall apart? Sandy soils feel gritty. Silty soils feel smooth – even soapy. Clay soils feel sticky. Decide what sort of soil you have got.

Shake a sample of soil up with water – perhaps in a coffee jar with a screw-top lid. Let the soil settle. What do you notice? If you can, shake up two different samples of soil – of the same amount – and look for differences.

What floats? What sinks? Does the sinking material form layers? Draw your soil 'profile'.

Wash your hands thoroughly after handling soil.

What to talk about:
Any gardening book will tell you which plants are suited to different types of soil. It will tell you about the acidity and alkalinity of different soils. It will tell you how different soils are treated to make them lighter or less acid. Discuss this with your child. They may think that plants will grow anywhere.

What to record:
Record the condition of your own garden soil. List some plants that will grow there. If you haven't a garden, plan a window-box. What soil will you use? What will you grow?

Draw your 'soil profile'. Label what you can.

Comment from parent or carer:

From the teacher:

The power of peat

Child's name:

Date activity set:

Date for returning this sheet to school:

To the parent or adult carer:
Peat is commonly added to garden soil to lighten it and to help it hold water. Peat may contain nutrients needed by plants. You will need a little peat-type material – bulb or potting compost will do.

There has been understandable concern about the indiscriminate use of natural peat damaging the environment. There are a number of peat substitutes, including those made from coconut shells.

Many children – and some adults – believe that plants 'feed' on the nutrients in soil. While they need tiny quantities of mineral salts, green plants make their own food and structure from water and carbon dioxide, using the power of the Sun.

What to do:
Peat and peat substitutes help the soil to hold water. You can test this for yourself. You will need a funnel and two measuring jugs. Do not use things that you also use for food. You can make both by cutting pop bottles in half. The top becomes the funnel; the base can be your measure. You will need two bases.

Put a measured amount of peat in the funnel. Put a measured amount of water in one jug. Pour the water slowly through the peat, catching what goes through in the second jug. If you measure the water that went through, and take that away from the amount you poured in, you have the amount the peat held back.

Compare this figure with your results using equal amounts of other soils.

What to talk about:
Why should soil hold water? What do the plants need the water for?
What other materials – potting composts and bulb fibres – hold water well?
When is it important to make the soil drain water better?

What to record:
Record the amounts of water retained by different soils.

Comment from parent or carer:

From the teacher:

Solid clay

Child's name:
_____

Date activity set:
_____

Date for returning this sheet to school:
_____

To the parent or adult carer:
Clay is a material that is made of fine mineral grains and water. You can mould clay. Dry clay keeps its shape, but breaks easily and is not waterproof. Baking clay in an oven changes it permanently into a material that is waterproof.

What to do:
Go on a clay hunt round your home. Look for things that started out as clay. Look especially in the bathroom; and don't forget the home itself – and the garden.

If you can, dig some clay from the ground. You may need to dig quite deep. Use it to model something. How strong is an air-dried model?

Use modelling clay to model something. Plasticine and other modelling 'clays' are not real clay. But they will make shapes, and some will dry in the air.

What to talk about:
The changes that take place. Clay can be pushed, pulled, twisted and squeezed. Changes of shape can be reversed. Dry clay may need water adding before it can be reshaped.

Compare a fired clay object – a pottery plant pot, for example – with soft clay. What are the differences?

What to record:
List all the clay objects you have found. Does your collection include the bathroom sink, cups and saucers, plant pots?

Describe the changes you saw when working with clay.

Comment from parent or carer:

From the teacher:

Bubbling and peeling

Child's name:

Date activity set:

Date for returning this sheet to school:

To the parent or adult carer:
The effects of the Sun and rain are all around us, damaging houses, paintwork, fences and garden furniture. You can expect more damage with greater exposure. Surprisingly, it is the Sun that causes the most damage, drying and splitting woodwork.

What to do:
Look around your home for damage from the Sun and from water. Can you find:

- fading paint?
- peeling paint?
- splitting wood?
- water damage?

How could you prevent this happening again?

Do you know how the sunlight strikes your home? How is the sunny side of your home different from the shaded side?

What to talk about:
Talk about all the ways you protect your home from Sun and water damage; how the roof, gutters and drain-pipes take the water away; how often you repaint; whether you oil or varnish wooden garden furniture, or creosote fences.

Maybe you have PVC or aluminium window frames; explain how these are corrosion proof.

What to record:
Sketch your home. On your drawing, mark in all the places where you saw Sun and water damage. Draw in how the Sun strikes your home.

Comment from parent or carer:

From the teacher:

Rotting and rusting

Child's name:

Date activity set:

Date for returning this sheet to school:

To the parent or adult carer:
Many metals corrode on exposure to water and the air. Iron and steel, which is made from iron, rust. Stainless steel is an alloy that does not rust. Children may think that rust is something that emerges from inside the nail; they may not know that air, as well as water, is needed for rusting.

What to do:
Test the effects of water on small metal objects. You could try nails, pins or paper clips. Rub them with sandpaper before you start to give them a shiny surface. How could you test your nails?

You might:

● put one in water;
● coat one in grease or Vaseline and put it in water;
● put one in cool water that has boiled in the kettle (boiling drives out all the air);
● paint one with oil paint, let it dry and put it in water.

How long will you leave your nails? Look at them every day. Which rust? Why is this?

What to talk about:
How you can stop nails rusting. What are the best treatments? Why do they work? Look at some galvanised nails. Staples, clout nails and felting nails may be coated with zinc, which prevents them rusting.

What to record:
What the nails look like, every few days.

Comment from parent or carer:

From the teacher:

The rustiest nail

Child's name:

Date activity set:

Date for returning this sheet to school:

To the parent or adult carer:
Children may believe that rusting is the result of something coming out of a metal, rather than the effects of water and oxygen on the surface.

This competition challenges their ideas by asking them to think about places where nails will rust.

What to do:
You are going to find the best place in your home for rusting. You can choose as many places as you have nails.

Take some steel nails. Rub them well with sandpaper so that all the surfaces are shiny.

Choose places where you think you will see plenty of rusting. Put one nail in each place.

Check your nails once a week.

What to talk about:
You might look around outside together for examples of rust – in fence posts, wire staples, gate hinges and cars. Why have they rusted as they have?

Suppose you put a galvanised, zinc-coated nail with each steel nail. What changes do you see in the galvanised nail? The zinc is not affected by the damp, and protects the steel underneath.

What to record:
Put your nails in order of rusting. Compare them with a new nail. Draw all the nails as they are, and explain why they may have rusted like that.

Comment from parent or carer:

From the teacher:

4   Seasons

Teachers' notes

Moving stars

One for the autumn or spring terms, when the evenings are fairly short and the skies can be clear. Warn the children against undertaking any outdoor activity like this after dark unless they have an adult with them. A camera with a shutter control gives you an opportunity to see the way the stars move.

Our nearest star

Even adults may not be aware that the Sun is a star. This activity – with its accompanying warning about looking at the Sun – shows how shadows change during the day. It can confirm quite the wrong idea – that the Sun is moving – and this is a tough concept to challenge, as Galileo found.

Our changing Moon

Observation of the Moon with binoculars is easy; but children are unlikely to get completely clear nights for all their Moon observations, and will have to guess at some. They will also notice that the Moon changes its position in the sky, and that it is quite frequently visible in daylight.

Fibres and fabrics

One for any season; in fact, one that could be done twice, to contrast the fabrics worn at different times of the year.

Bonfire night

Bonfires and fireworks are used to celebrate many different festivals as well as the Gunpowder Plot, and you can use the sheet on irreversible change as appropriate.

Autumn days

An opportunity to understand more about the process of decay and the recycling of materials.

Spring morning

A chance to see the changes that take place in this season, and to understand that even things that are apparently dead may be only dormant.

Festival candles

Candles make a fascinating study of change, and of states of matter. Safety warnings, of course.

Summer holidays

Weather is not necessarily a science topic, but weather records allow long-term observation.

Back to school

An autumn term activity to record reducing day length and to compare this with the apparent movement of the Sun.

Our changing Moon

Child's name:

Date activity set:

Date for returning this sheet to school:

To the parent or adult carer:
You can observe the Moon best on autumn or spring nights. Autumn is better, since it gets dark more quickly. Inevitably, some nights will be too cloudy for you to see the Moon properly, but the next clear night will help you to work out what you have missed.

The Moon has no light of its own. It reflects the light from the Sun. As the Moon moves around the Earth, the lighted area and the area of shadow change. These give the monthly phases of the Moon.

What to do:
Use a large round coin to draw thirty circles on the back of this sheet.

Every clear night, go out together and record the shape of the Moon. Write the date under each drawing.

Notice how the Moon changes through a month.

What to talk about:
The 'smallest' Moon is called the new Moon; the largest, 'full Moon'. A book will help you with other descriptions – waxing, waning, gibbous.

Think of all the ways the Moon affects our lives – the tides, moonlight, stories about people affected by the Moon.

What to record:
The phases of the Moon on the back of this sheet. You could cut a picture like this into squares, with the Moon in the centre of each square. If you staple the squares together, they will make a flick book showing the changing Moon.

Comment from parent or carer:

From the teacher:

Moving stars

Child's name:

Date activity set:

Date for returning this sheet to school:

To the parent or adult carer:
You will need a clear night for this investigation. Binoculars can be useful.

What to do:
On a clear night, look at the stars. Give your eyes time to accommodate to the dark – several minutes. The longer they are in the dark, the more you will be able to see. Estimate the number of stars you can see. There are millions more that you can't see because they aren't bright enough for your eyes.

Try to spot the Plough – a group of stars that most people can recognise. The handle of the Plough leads your eye towards the pole star, Polaris. Watch out for artificial satellites. These are single points of light that cruise at a steady pace in straight lines across the sky. Look out for planets. You may see a hint of colour – green on Venus, red on Mars.

What to talk about:
The number and beauty of the stars. Although they appear to be in groups, they may be huge distances apart in depth. You may see white areas – almost like a chiffon scarf – on a very clear night. These areas are part of our own galaxy – the Milky Way.

What to record:
Write a letter to your friend, saying when they should go out and look at the stars.

Comment from parent or carer:

From the teacher:

Our nearest star

Child's name:

Date activity set:

Date for returning this sheet to school:

To the parent or adult carer:
The most important lesson to come from this activity is never to look at the Sun. Damage to the retina need only take a moment, and can be permanent. Don't be tempted to look at the Sun through anything – sunglasses, photograph negatives – even on a cloudy day.

The Sun is our nearest star. Without its light and heat, there would be no life on Earth. The sheet describes a safe way of making observations.

What to do:
Which is your sunniest window? Does it cast shadows into the room? Do those shadows change during the day?

Draw a cat and a mouse (or something similar) onto cardboard. Cut them out. Use Blu-tack or tape to stick the cat to the window so that it casts a shadow on the wall.

Guessing time. Stick the mouse to the wall where you think the cat's shadow will be, later.

Observe what happens. Check from time to time. Were you right? If not, try again.

What to talk about:
The Sun appears to move across the sky; but it is the turning of the Earth that gives this movement. This is hard to believe.

What to record:
Draw your investigation. Record the results on the back of this paper.

Comment from parent or carer:

From the teacher:

Fibres and fabrics

Child's name:

Date activity set:

Date for returning this sheet to school:

To the parent or adult carer:
Few clothes – even those made at home – are made with just one fibre. Most are mixtures of fibres, giving, for example, the coolness of cotton and the crease-resistance of nylon.

The labels on clothes give some idea of the fibres they are made from.

What to do:
Look for labels on your favourite clothes. What fibres are they made from? Why were these fibres chosen?

List all the different fibre names you can find. Divide your list into natural fibres and those made by people.

What to talk about:
Some fibres are natural. Others are artificial. The number of artificial fibres is increasing all the time – look for new fibres like ICI's Tencel.

Discuss the other logos you find on labels – dry clean only, washing temperature, etc.

What to record:
Draw your favourite clothes. Next to each drawing, write the fibre from which the clothing was made.

Comment from parent or carer:

From the teacher:

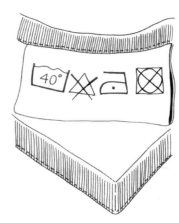

Bonfire night

Child's name:

Date activity set:

Date for returning this sheet to school:

To the parent or adult carer:
Bonfire night offers lots of examples of irreversible change. The bonfire embers can't be returned to wood; the spent rockets can't become new fireworks.

This may seem obvious to you, but understanding that some changes are temporary and some permanent is an important stage in children's preparation for chemistry.

What to do:
On bonfire night, look around for examples of changes. You could use a picture of bonfire night to help you. Which of these changes are permanent? Which are temporary?

What to talk about:
Use the opportunity to define permanent and temporary – or irreversible and reversible. Think of examples of both. Mixing salt and water is reversible – you can get the salt and the water back; burning a candle is irreversible – the candle is permanently changed.

What to record:
Illustrate the back of this sheet with examples of reversible and irreversible change. You could draw, write or cut pictures from a newspaper or catalogue.

Comment from parent or carer:

From the teacher:

Autumn days

Child's name:

Date activity set:

Date for returning this sheet to school:

To the parent or adult carer:
This is an activity that encourages children to look more closely at the changing seasons, and in particular to observe that decay is an important part of the cycle of life. Go out somewhere near home where there is evidence of the changing seasons. You don't need much – a corner with a few rotting leaves will do.

It's an activity for the autumn.

What to do:
Look for evidence of autumn: falling leaves; sycamore helicopters; conkers; even safe fungi. Collect some fallen leaves.

What will happen to all these things? Why aren't they there in the spring? Some are swept up; but the rest will rot.

What use are rotting leaves? Can you grow plants in them? What will happen to these plants next autumn?

What to talk about:
The cycle of decay, which turns rotting leaves to compost ready for next year. The fact that it is bacteria and other micro-organisms that cause the leaves to rot. They are not just 'germs'.

What to record:
A gardener has a garden full of leaves. Tell her what will happen to them. Tell her how useful they can be.

Comment from parent or carer:

From the teacher:

Spring morning

Child's name:

Date activity set:

Date for returning this sheet to school:

To the parent or adult carer:
Take a walk on a spring morning. Look for signs of new life. Notice how these result from what at first sight appears dead – bulbs, seeds, buds.

What to do:
Spot seeds growing. Sycamore helicopters and others will germinate on the ground.

Spot bulbs shooting. Crocus, snowdrops and daffodils will be growing from dry, brown bulbs.

Spot buds bursting. Most trees and shrubs will be carrying leaf buds.

What to talk about:
How life processes slowed during the winter; how natural processes go on slowly, waiting for the warmth and light that comes in the spring.

What to record:
It's winter, and your friend has an old tree in his garden. 'It's dead,' he says. 'There are no leaves on it; only brown buds and dry seeds. We're going to cut it down.' Tell him why not to, using the back of this paper.

How do you know it is still alive?

Comment from parent or carer:

From the teacher:

Festival candles

Child's name:

Date activity set:

Date for returning this sheet to school:

To the parent or adult carer:
It's important to teach young children about safety with flames. You must decide whether you do this activity as a demonstration, or allow your child to light the candle under your supervision. It may be appropriate to teach about lighting matches by striking away from your face; to demonstrate how holding the lighted match under the candle wick lights it, and to show how to put out a lighted candle.

In any event, secure the candle upright, make sure that hair and sleeves cannot hang in the flame, and do not encourage carrying a lit candle around.

What to do:
YOU MUST NOT DO THIS ACTIVITY WITHOUT AN ADULT.

Fix a candle upright, and light it. Look carefully at the candle flame. How many colours do you see? What does the wick look like? Where does the tip of the wick burn away?

Draw the candle flame carefully on the back of this sheet. Use colours to label the different parts.

Put the candle out, several times over, in different ways. Explain why the candle is going out.

What to talk about:
The different parts of a candle flame show solids, liquids and gases. The candle is solid. The melting wax is liquid. The part that burns – blue and yellow – is gaseous. Think about the different ways of putting the candle out. Blowing it would seem to add more air – in fact it blows the gas away – taking away the fuel. Pinching the flame cuts the fuel off from oxygen. Snuffing the flame does the same. Flames also go out in very cold conditions.

What to record:
Draw your candle flame on the back of this sheet, and label the parts.

Comment from parent or carer:

From the teacher:

Summer holidays

Child's name:

Date activity set:

Date for returning this sheet to school:

To the parent or adult carer:
This is a sheet to complete through the summer holiday. It records the weather at a time of the year when we can often expect extremes – drought, thunderstorms, early mists.

A record of the weather is useless in itself. What is important is to notice the changes brought about by, and related to, the weather.

What to do:
Write the dates of your summer holidays on the back of this sheet. List every day. Record the weather on each day.

Next to each day, record something you saw that was linked to the weather. It might be forked lightning, or dried-out grass.

What to talk about:
Discuss the change that the hot weather makes. Speculate on the ways that animals survive summer weather. Find out what you can.

Notice how some plants are dried out – even killed – by hot weather. Others survive, and stay green. A lawn will often give good examples. Shallow-rooted grass turns brown; but deep-rooted dandelions draw water from far under the ground and stay green.

What to record:
A daily weather record.

Comment from parent or carer:

From the teacher:

Back to school

Child's name:

Date activity set:

Date for returning this sheet to school:

To the parent or adult carer:
This is a sheet about day length. When children return to school in the autumn, the days are getting shorter. This is due to the tilt of the Earth, which turns us more away from the Sun in the autumn and winter months. The children notice the change in dark mornings and evenings. As Christmas approaches, they may go to school and come home in the dark.

What to do:
Look in the newspaper for sunrise and sunset times. These are often near the weather forecast. Look on several days, and record the times on this sheet. Notice how they change.

Record how light it is first thing in the morning, and when you come home from school. Why do you play out less on autumn evenings?

Notice the change in the clocks. What is it meant to do? What does it mean to you? How does it change your life?

What to talk about:
The changes in day length, and the way that the days get shorter from the longest day – around June 21st – and longer from the shortest – December 21st.

Precautions that arise from the early darkness: bicycle lights; reflective clothing; being taken to school and collected.

What to record:
Write a story about school on one of the short autumn days.

Comment from parent or carer:

From the teacher:

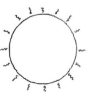

5 Forces

Teachers' notes

Top toy

Most schools introduce activities about toys running down slopes at some point. The behaviour of a free-running vehicle is complex; many forces are taking effect, including gravity and friction. The main focus of this sheet is not on forces, but on fair testing; and the results are not as important as the technique. Look for evidence that the importance of repeating the investigation is understood; it should be clear that it is being repeated to establish the validity of the results.

Bouncing balls

Once again, the forces involved are complex. The important thing is to look at prediction – prediction based on previous experience; prediction that develops as children increase the range of their experiences. How far do the results match the predictions?

Frisbee fling

This is a nice activity for investigation. There are so many possible changes that can be made. The issue of 'best' may arise. What is the best Frisbee? The answer is that it depends upon your parameters – best might be the one that flies furthest; or most smoothly; or accurately hits a target. You will have to decide.

Parachute practice

The parachute can be varied in many ways – the way it is launched, the height it is launched from, its size and weight. Use this as a basis for discussing the control and changing of variables. If you changed both the size and the weight at once, could you tell the effect each was having?

Kite flight

This kite design is very reliable, but some wind is needed. The forces involved – the wind, the tug of the string, the weight of the kite – are resolved to allow the kite to fly.

Top toy

Child's name:

Date activity set:

Date for returning this sheet to school:

To the parent or adult carer:
Most children will have moving toys. This sheet invites them to compare the toys' movement. They might set free-running toys off down a ramp; or race powered toys against each other.

The activity introduces ideas about timing, measuring and recording.

What to do:
Set up a ramp. A plank, or even a big book, on a pile of books will do.

Set your free-running toys off down the ramp. Which goes furthest? Why? Does it always go furthest?

Compare wind-up toys by giving each three winds. How far does each toy go on three winds?

Compare electrical toys by setting up start and finish lines. Use a watch to see which covers the whole racetrack in the shortest time.

What to talk about:
Talk about fairness. Are the tests fair? Is each toy given an equal chance to perform?

Talk about recording. Should each test be done more than once? Why?

What to record:
You could make a graph of your results on the back of this page. Compare each toy against its performance.

Comment from parent or carer:

From the teacher:

Bouncing balls

Child's name:

Date activity set:

Date for returning this sheet to school:

To the parent or adult carer:
Different balls bounce to different heights. The ball, the height from which it is dropped, and the surface you drop it on are all factors in this. If you change one of these – you use different balls, for example – you should keep the drop height and the surface the same.

Why balls bounce differently is not apparent from observation. Higher bouncing balls regain their shape quickly.

What to do:
Make a collection of balls. Decide how you are going to measure the bounce. Will it be to the top of the ball? Compare the bounce, marking the heights on the wall.

Try the same ball, dropped from different heights. How close to the dropping height will the ball get?

Try the same ball, dropped from the same height, onto different surfaces. What difference does that make?

What to talk about:
This is a great activity for prediction – 'I think that one will bounce highest' – but this should not lead to fiddling the results.

Discuss how far the results matched the predictions. Why do you think this is?

What to record:
Results could be recorded as a table – or in a graph.

Comment from parent or carer:

From the teacher:

Frisbee fling

Child's name:

Date activity set:

Date for returning this sheet to school:

To the parent or adult carer:
The reasons why Frisbees and boomerangs fly are very complex; but that doesn't stop us using them for an investigation of flight.

If you don't have a Frisbee, use an ice cream container lid. For a boomerang, strap two rulers together at right angles.

Use these well away from other people.

What to do:
Investigate the flight of your Frisbee or boomerang. In a very open space, aim for the longest flight – both distance and number of seconds in the air. What ensures a good flight?

Put a target on the ground. A sheet of newspaper or a coat will do. See how accurately you can throw the Frisbee or boomerang. Find the best way to throw it for happy landings.

What to talk about:
What makes the boomerang or Frisbee fly well? Is it the angle you launch it, the power you put in, how you hold your arm?

What to record:
Record your throws and results – how far, how long, whether you hit the target. Your friend wants to know how to win a Frisbee throwing competition. Write a note explaining the best way of throwing one.

Comment from parent or carer:

From the teacher:

Parachute practice

Child's name:

Date activity set:

Date for returning this sheet to school:

To the parent or adult carer:
You are going to investigate a model parachute. It doesn't matter whether you make your parachute from cloth or tissue paper, as long as it is symmetrical, and you don't overload it.

Parachutes drift down because of the friction of air moving across the surface. It isn't just that the canopy fills with air, as you would expect when you think about bell-shaped balloons with holes in and sports parachutes without a 'bell'.

Teach children not to climb or lean from anywhere dangerous to launch their parachute.

What to do:
Make a parachute from a big handkerchief or a square of tissue paper. Tie a thin thread to each corner, and tie the four ends together. Find a weight that will let the parachute fall slowly. A Plasticine ball can be made bigger and smaller.

Fold the parachute so that the weight is on the inside, and throw it up from the ground. Practise until the parachute drifts really well.

Now test your parachute. What is the longest time it will stay up? Can you change the parachute to make it stay up longer? Can you throw it so that it always lands in a target area?

What to talk about:
How parachutes fly. The balance between the weight and the size of the canopy. Real parachutes have a central hole to stop the parachutist swinging. If you can, make a hole in the parachute and explore the difference it makes.

What to record:
Draw your most successful parachute on the back of this paper. Record some advice to parachutists.

Comment from parent or carer:

From the teacher:

Kite flight

Child's name:

Date activity set:

Date for returning this sheet to school:

To the parent or adult carer:
A simple kite made from a plastic supermarket bag and two garden sticks can be very successful.

Kites fly because of a balance of forces – the push of the wind, the pull of the string, and the downward drag of gravity.

Fly your kite on a breezy day. DO NOT fly it near roads, rail lines or overhead power lines.

What to do:
Slit open a supermarket bag and tape two thin garden sticks to it. Tie four thin strings as a harness, and attach a tail made from newspaper. Tie a long string to the harness.

Launch the kite with the wind behind you. Tug gently and evenly to help it soar. Explore the effects of changing the kite. Does it fly better with holes cut in it – or with a longer or shorter tail?

What to talk about:
How kites fly. How to ensure a really successful flight. The changes you could make to the kite.

You might try making a bigger or smaller kite, scaling it up or down.

What to record:
Draw your best kite. Explain to someone else how to make and fly a good kite.

Comment from parent or carer:

From the teacher: